ADDiCTiON 2.0

THE DEMISE OF THE INTELLECT
WITH POETIC AMBIENCE

MINDSTIR MEDIA

INTRODUCTION

Addiction has reached epidemic proportions in our country these days. Anyone who is addicted or has a loved one who suffers from addiction will benefit greatly from the information contained in this publication. Unknown most, addiction has many forms, faces and faucets, a lot of which will be described in detail. Alcoholism and addiction are very personal to me, as it has both consumed and ultimately taken both of my parents' lives. Besides having its way with me for many years, causing sheer destruction to me and my loved ones personally, financially and especially emotionally, it is truly nothing more than a waste of time, energy, money and precious life. This is designed to help people understand the nature of addiction more, how it works to destroy you, what it will do to your life, and finally, how to stop it.

Addiction is a very complex disease, and one that doesn't come with an owner's manual, so I felt the need to warn others of the dangers that lie ahead of them if they wish to continue down the road of addiction. This road is paved with a lot of good people's souls. I can assure you this, with as much certainty that the sun will probably rise some time tomorrow morning, that you will indeed, beyond the shadow of any doubt, go through all the trials and tribulations depicted in this book in one way, shape or form if you continue down that road. This isn't intended to scare anyone, but rather to bring attention to the soul stealing disease of addiction that America seems to now be riddled with. Recovering from addiction is probably the hardest thing (mentally) you'll ever have to do in your life. The choice is obvious; keep using or stop. But, a healthy fear of the unknown has kept many firmly in place. This will shine light into the dark corners of addiction for all to see. I don't like being lied to, therefore I won't sugarcoat anything. I will be cut and dry, which is the best way to handle this situation. The only things needed for recovery are an open mind, determination and information. The truth will always prevail. Included after the fourth chapter is a collection of very special poems I've written in prison when getting sober. I must warn you, these poems are addictive as well.

CHAPTER ONE

ATTITUDES, EMOTIONS AND BEHAVIORS

How you act outwardly is in direct reflection to how you feel on the inside. This is the addicts biggest hurtle to get over, and also the biggest piece of the puzzle. This is of critical importance for anyone who wishes to recover from being addicted to drugs, alcohol or any other mind-altering substance. This will make or break your recovery attempt, for sure. I've seen a lot of people stumped on this one, myself included, for many painful years. As humans, we're flexible and have the freedom of choice (thank the Republicans). So is the same with our attitudes. We choose how we feel (unless we suffer from anxiety, depression or other mood-altering conditions). Contrary to popular belief, no one can make you do anything, unless of course it's paying taxes, and some people don't even do that. A certain reverend from New York comes to mind. This, in itself, is an addiction to oneself or the epitome of greed. This Chapter will outline the basic and common behavior associated with addiction, with greed being the biggest motive. We choose our attitudes; they're not hereditary or one size fits all. As adults, we choose the attitude to best fit the situation we find ourselves in. As addicts, we use our attitudes as tools of unwitting self-destruction, caring only about ourselves and our own needs. It is important to note here that once the attitude is conceived and formed, the behavior will soon follow. It's only a matter of time and twisted mental thought until this attitude will manifest itself into your behavior. This formula applies to everyone, not just addicts. It is quite apparent that this is usually how bad things happen. In the heat of the moment, we decide with our emotions and make a snap decision. We have to go with it now, as the wheels are already in motion. Good, bad or indifferent, we have to live with the consequences of our actions. it's easy to see how having a bad attitude can be harmful to us in the long run.

Robert Christopher Padmore

The addictive personality is unsatisfiable, it spends every waking moment (conscious of not) pursuing the object of its desire, or drug of choice. We will think of how we will do it, when or where we will do it, or with whoever else we could possibly do it with, literally obsessing over it until we finally do it. This is the basic and common mindset of an addict. Besides thinking of how we can screw the next guy out of some cash, to buy more drugs, the addicted mind is always thinking and pondering new ways to scam people. Many will play upon others sympathy, presenting some poor, unfortunate soul's story. Homeless, no job, no food, a story as old as time itself, just to get a few more dollars to buy more drugs. But this doesn't happen overnight. The addict will think they are getting better at what they do, and become more daring, egotistical and arrogant as time goes on, and this will usually end in one of two ways. Either the law gets involved in our debacle and we end up in jail, through a series of really stupid decisions, followed by some really stupid consequences, or we are found out and our cover is blown, leaving us susceptible to our scam-ee's wrath. But as I've said, it starts out so slowly and gradually that you don't even notice it. First you will start to show the symptoms of addiction. Impatience and annoyance will become two feelings synonymous with being alive. Everything will irritate you, we become very impatient. The only thing that will make us feel better is indulgence in our addiction. Over the years, these two feelings will multiply and gain strength in the addict, eventually to take over the addict's mind and ruin their life, and usually everyone else's around them or related to them. But hey, we're just trying to have a good time. And that's all well and good for some people, but before you know it, your drug of choice is becoming involved in everything you do. Let's say you're late for work because a bad hangover slowed you down, or sick from an excess of drugs\alcohol from the night before. These are the stepping stones across the river of addiction. Many people find themselves in this perilous situation. And the funny thing about it is, we're not all prone to this disease. Some get it, and some don't. Nevertheless, it's good to know where you stand, especially when it comes to this, because if you don't, you might find yourself with a lifetime of misery and unhappiness, all brought on by none other than yourself!

Habitual thinking has put blinders on us. We only see one way of doing things. Soon we will have only one emotion left; anger. The only time we will be happy is when we can use, otherwise we're just angry it wasn't enough, or didn't last long enough, or happen soon enough, or be good enough, or just angry that we can't use when we want to. In a nutshell, this is addiction. The seemingly endless annoying rut we have somehow managed to get ourselves into. The attitude is key here, as we have control over at least that. With a little strength, we can develop the right one. However, fostering the right attitude can prove a challenge for the addict. We do things one way, and change does not come easy sometimes, especially when we don't really want to deep down inside. Another key here, self-honesty is of the utmost importance. You can fool anyone, but when you fool yourself, the consequences can be dire. This is exactly why the addict has to be the one to initiate the change in themselves. Nothing will stick if it's done for any other reason. Not a girlfriend, spouse, job or anything. Only for the reason that the addict seeks a better life. Denial should be mentioned here, as this is the addicts sharpened sword, ready to cut down any vines growing in our garden of Eden. The amount of denial you will go through will depend on your depth of character, or your ability to be honest with yourself. This is exactly why it's good to have a higher power, or belief in God, because if you don't believe in anything (A God of some sort), there's no reason to be honest or even civil towards one another. Chaos and anarchy will rule the streets, and there will be much civil unrest as man's addictive nature spills over into his emotions and threatens to annihilate life as we know it. Sounds crazy, right? The fact is, we're all susceptible to addiction if we're exposed to it for a long enough period of time.

We grieve the loss of our addiction, just like that of a loved one. We think about it constantly, even dream about it in the chronic stages. This is how far our addiction has grown; now it's in our subconscious mind! And anyone who knows how the mind works knows that the subconscious runs all of our facilities without us even knowing it, like our breathing, reflexes and central nervous system and other things to help keep us alive. So, now we can add addiction to that list as well. This is very dangerous territory, and masses of people are headed that way. This will have dire consequences on our society and in families across the country. Addicts aren't very good at accepting responsibility for their problems and will blame any and everything for being the reason that they used in the first place. Make no mistake here, the addict is actually

Robert Christopher Padmore

fooling him\herself into believing that some outside entity or event is actually the reason behind their continued use. Not a bad argument, for a child. As addicts, we are very much like that of a child; king baby to be exact. This is how addictive behavior and interests manifests itself into an individual. You can see it in their attitude; it's always me, me, me. Always very grandiose and full of themselves, usually boasting about themselves, and will never see the other side of things. No matter what, right now we are knee deep in this problem as a country. It's quite obvious with the behavior of the NFL during the kneeling controversy and the women's soccer team, of course. That coupled with the extremely biased mainstream media, not to mention the democrats themselves and all of their baggage they drag around everywhere. It's interesting to look at these scandals and how we hop from one crisis to another, it's these same cable news shows that shape and perpetuate all of these king baby ideas, allowing them to flourish, develop and grow. This behavior is not only toxic, but self-serving as well as self-destructive. Though emboldened with arrogance and self-righteous anger, these people care of nothing but their ultimate goal, to destroy all of mankind, from the inside out and one by one.

Anger should be addressed immediately. This is a certain emotion the addict needs to learn to stay away from. However, this will prove to be an uphill battle as anger has become one of the addict's favorite tools, used at his\her own discretion, for the obvious reason of perpetuating our addiction longer. It should be said here that, over time, anger itself can become an addiction as well. Sometimes we feel very powerful when angry, especially for passionate people. The blood pressure goes up, we enter euphoric anger, when you feel energized and light-headed. It really is a buzz in itself. Once you feel it for a long enough period of time, and with a little self-honesty, you can see it for yourself. I was addicted to anger myself when I was younger. I've many scars, a shattered metatarsal, and high blood pressure all of my life. These are the physical manifestations of harboring anger.

Just as we have engraved our own way into our minds, it has its way of engraving itself into us as well, and in many ways; physical, mental and emotional. The emotional part can be especially painful, as well as dangerous to your mental health. A lot of people push the emotions so far that there's no coming back, and they end up on the fifth floor of the local hospital. I was there too. Alcohol has a way of displacing morals and values, just like any other addiction. An addict's anger and being too in touch with our emotions will always cause problems for us because we don't know when to stop. Anger is a valid feeling, but one that we have manipulated and capitalized on to use at our own liking at any given time. This, in itself, is the epitome of addiction. Addicts are masters of the emotions and will use them with much malice to get what they want. Addicts care nothing of other's feelings; only their own feelings matter. We have become true masters of manipulating our own as well as other's feelings. We are merely acting out our own selfish desires in the theatre we make.

The brain is a very fertile place; all kinds of thoughts can grow. If given negative thoughts, the result will be just that, negative. It's important to note that negative thoughts pile up. The addict will just stuff these feelings and disregard the thought, thinking 'once I forget them, they won't bother me.' But much like how someone drops the charges against you in a court of law, the state will pick them up and charge you with it anyway. Almost in the same way, the thought will stay in the back of your mind, multiply and gain strength until they explode in our heads and come out in a negative fashion, usually at the wrong time and place, causing further problems for us. At this point, it's easy to see how having the wrong attitude or a bad attitude can be harmful to us. Once in recovery, negative thoughts are replaced with positive ones, so the end result can be just that; positive! So how the attitude is, the behavior is soon to follow.

CHAPTER TWO

IN REALITY

Dysfunction and dishonesty have become commonplace in today's society. Unfortunately, dysfunction sells. It's the narrative of most sitcoms, as well as a "clever" marketing strategy for people who value money more than morals and values. Someone who would sell their soul to the devil for monetary gain. The fact is, most people don't care at all about others; they just want your money. Nowadays, we have all kinds of flavored beers, high energy alcohol and caffeine drinks that can potentially stop your heart, as well as energy shots for those who had a little too much sauce last night.

The businesses are gearing up with shiny new products for a new generation to wreck your lives in a not so new way. It's actually the same way man has been making life hard for himself since the beginning of time, or at least since we've been making alcohol. Addiction is commonplace in today's society, with all of the new technology we've experienced in the last twenty years, of course everyone's addicted. We all like to make things easier, and they should be easier, as we are busy and don't have time for this nonsense! This is the basic and common attitude of a lot of people these days, and it reflects just how clueless we are about addiction in society. The above scenario is fodder for addiction, the perfect place and mindset to support a healthy addiction.

What was once called King Baby syndrome will be discussed here, as this attitude is prevalent and displayed brazenly by many professional athletes, as well as movie stars and pop culture icons here in America, who a lot of children, pre-teens and teenagers idolize and want to be like. Only responsible parents can truly appreciate the obvious problem here. King Baby wants what he wants and he wants it now! No matter the cost, all bullshit aside, it's about me and I don't care about your feelings. This self-serving personality disorder is alive and well in America, and threatening to tear apart the social fabric so carefully woven together by the souls of forgotten soldiers so long ago. This personality disorder can become an addiction in itself. if left unchecked, it feeds off of itself in a strange way and will ultimately lead to their own self-destruction, but only after years of mental suffering, anguish and actual self-inflicted pain, just like any other addict. The only tools we have to battle King Baby syndrome are common sense and maturity. Please note, addictions aren't only limited to drugs and alcohol. There's also, laziness, sex, food, money, power, control and fame, just to name a few, as well as a slew of personality disorders that come with each one. These disorders are all evil and self-serving. Of course everyone needs food, and to have sex and money once in a while would be nice also, but when taken to the extreme, these selfish desires for more, more, more will only serve to make your life miserable in a multitude of ways. Kind of like what people consider to be karma. And this will happen over and over again, until the behavior is ceased.

In today's society, dysfunction is celebrated to much applause and viewership on cable network news channels and especially on shows like The View, Jerry Springer and the like. It also crept into the National Football League, as well as the women's Olympic Team, headed, of course, by late night comedians, who have taken all of the humor out of their jokes and replaced it with one sided political rhetoric. These people above are the ones who live behind walls in gated communities, telling the rest of us that walls are immoral and ineffective. So, this is today's late-night television, aimed at the youth of America, as grandma and grandpa are usually in bed by 10:00 PM. These shows are acceptable for our younger viewers to watch? They are effectively spawning a new generation of hate filled, narcissistic, holier than thou people with a 'who cares about the next guy' attitude. If we wish to call ourselves a civilized society, respect must be exercised, and here's the thing, it must also be earned. There's more on respect in Chapter 4. Since we're speaking of respect, I'd like to say here that Christmas, December 25th, is actually the birthday of Jesus Christ. Although a lot of people claim to not believe in him, this is the most widespread observance of any holiday, even making the day after Thanksgiving the first day of the holiday shopping season. But do non-believers partake in the exchanging of gifts? This is exactly what makes America, America. You can celebrate any holiday you like, or none at all. But it is important to recognize, we need to have respect for others if we want to be respected ourselves.

So, it seems in today's society we've learned nothing from our parents, grandparents and so on. If we have, most don't exercise it. In a world of voice commanded computers and remote control everything, things have been made so easy for us, by rights we should be living the life of Reilly. But as addicts, we always find new ways to make things hard for ourselves. The seven deadly sins are written all over dysfunctional behavior, yet some people live to be dysfunctional. These are the still sick and suffering, it's on the TV, the news, on the highways, and even in the supermarkets, or whenever a career politician speaks. What I don't understand is, if the seven deadly sins are such a trap, just waiting to swallow people's lives, they should be taught in school! An interesting point, because if they're not taught at home, and children grow up watching TV, literally absorbing and internalizing all of this dysfunction, not only in TV, let's face it, dysfunction becomes the new norm. And it's everywhere, however just like it's written in the bible, no good deed shall go undone. This negative behavior will be rewarded in the exact same way, negative. As you can never get something positive from something negative. This should be obvious. The likes of anger and irritability will taint your personality, frustration you will embrace wholeheartedly, never understanding the reason behind it, which will in turn drive your ignorance deeper. I used to say, "I'm Irish and I have a black cloud hanging over my head!" But the harsh truth is, after a lifetime of negativity, I only got more negativity. Christianity is the only religion that doesn't push things upon people. By that I mean you decide how deeply you wish to be involved, attending church on a weekly basis is all that is required of you. Christianity is a faith-based religion that deals with the virtues of people who are trying to follow the teachings of Jesus Christ. They certainly wouldn't kill you if you disagree with them, or do anything to harm you. The fact is, Christians are known for helping people in places like the food pantry, soup kitchens and helping families in need.

It isn't until we can become totally honest with ourselves and true to ourselves that things will begin to change. A lot is to be learned here, as an excess in any one of our feelings\emotions concerning pride, laziness, greed, vengeance, lust, gluttony or envy can prove to be life altering and only cause conflict and emotional instability. Alcohol is made for one reason, to make us feel good. And if one can make you feel like this, imagine what four or five would be like? This is alcoholic thinking at its finest, and also man's greatest downfall. Apply this train of thought to money, politics, fame, sexual deviance or even the control freak, and you have a full blown addict. How dangerous is this? Imagine, at all levels of the United States government. Everyone has the potential. This is exactly why I don't trust career politicians. The fact is, we are all human, and we all want to feel good. But being creatures of habit, we can't help ourselves and continue this behavior until it's too late. Most people don't think they are an alcoholic and many people believe they can stop anytime they want to. I beg to differ. To me, the proof is in the pudding. Has alcohol or any one of our drugs of choice ever got us into trouble? Whether it be personally, emotionally, financially or the big one, lawfully? if your answer is yes, then my friend, you are an addict and have officially crossed the invisible line between being normal and the vast wasteland of addiction. I might add here that this line is totally invisible and can only be seen and appreciated for what it is in hindsight. In other words, you don't know until it's too late. This is brought to our attention only in recovery because denial runs very deep in our veins. This isn't intended to spark the anger of anyone, be it as it may, this addictive nature has become so commonplace in today's society that it needs to be pointed out, addressed, and dealt with in a civilized way. That is if we don't wish to implode ourselves with our own selfish carnal desires.

Even as we engage one another in grocery stores or the laundromats, we are very aware of who is around us. This heightened sense of awareness is no doubt because of recent tragedies involving self-righteous anger and of course the new coronavirus. So, we're all aware of explosive behavior, and try not to make eye contact because everyone has the potential. In short, we're scared to death of each other. This reminds me of being in prison, New York State prison, chock full of murderers, rapists, and pedophiles. Here a man's true personality shines, as there are no material things to indulge in or hide behind. You're all the same, wearing state greens with a number on it. The only difference is the number. As we have all had our pride, ego, feelings of self-worth, and freedom taken from us in one swift blow, then thrown into general population and expected to get along and not cause any problems. However rough and rigid this seems is nothing in comparison to how it works, as long as there is an armed guard every fifty to sixty feet. The potential for sudden violence is in the air at all times, and given the ego and intelligence of the common criminal, fights are widespread and the stress can be mentally challenging. But honestly, I believe going to prison was a first class lesson on humility, and a certain level of humility must exist in every one of us in order to live a peaceful, harmoniously balanced life.

Personally, I believe the last administration of the United States has brought us to walking on eggshells, with the frivolous lawsuits and people being offended over everything. Some only looking to cause a problem because they seem to love problems. The way a certain reverend from New York was a guest of the white house at the same time that he owed twenty years of back taxes? It seems the old P.O.T.U.S wasn't too worried about rooting out corruption. This man stokes the flames of hatred after a family tragedy, then he literally, and figuratively, lives off of their grief. The perversion of the mind is a soul sickness seemingly spreading across America like that of a mental plague, threatening to extinguish our very existence, but only through our minds, in a very painful emotional way. Enough can never be said about the perversion of thoughts, as they lead to the perversion of actions, and in turn, lead to devastation in our communities in one way, shape or form mentally, physically and spiritually. The evils of negative thinking are outlined here and should be as obvious to you as the nose on your face. But for the addict, this is our comfortability zone. A literal playground of evil thoughts, deeds and desires. All serving one purpose, to keep us happy and addicted. So, addiction is bound to our souls forever once melded with these soul stealing feeling\emotions? Never say never, as a man, I can tell you anything broken can be fixed, as long as you have the time, tools, and interest to fix it! One would think that it should be of the utmost importance to want to fix yourself, but the addict feels they are not broken and work just fine. You can kind of see the mental back and forth the addict goes through, only to give in to ourselves, because that is what we really want anyway. And this happens over and over again, year after year, bringing untold mental anguish and suffering to the addict until he\she smartens up, or dies. Even jails and institutions have no effect on us. We will simply do our time and return to our old lifestyle. Sometimes it's all that we know.

CHAPTER THREE

POLITICAL ADDICTION

As I've said, addiction is very personal to me. My parents came to this country after World War II through Ellis island. I'm proud of my heritage, as everyone should be, but also proud of the fact that I was born here in America, land of the free, because it's the home of the brave. The place I grew up in. I will forever love this country, including all of the people in it. Though we are all free to choose our own opinion, everyone here in America should know about political addiction.

Though I'm no expert on politics, I have become very aware of the potential for bad things to happen. All you have to do is watch the news for five minutes to see the political circus that's happening in our nation's capital right now. It's dragged through the news everyday with addiction coming in a close second as shown by the recent sexual harassment scandals and the #MeToo movement. Imagine that, a whole movement of people all sexually harassed or raped by their bosses, co-workers, or people trying to "help" them. I think it's important to note here that this movement started in the entertainment industry and Hollywood. Both of these are ran by the left, Democrats or liberals, whichever label you prefer, who by Google definition are willing to disregard traditional values. This is called an oxymoron. If you're willing to disregard traditional values, then rape and lawlessness should be o.k. as we would be back in the caveman days. Since addiction is alive, well and obviously thriving in our nation's capital, as clearly shown by the 2016 presidential election, most Americans now know, politicians are liars. The worst of liars. They say what they say about a multitude of things, but once they're elected, they do nothing. These people have the best jobs on earth, with untold of benefits. This is the exact reason why career politicians exist. These people need someone to oversee their work, as their districts lay in ruin, poverty and homelessness run rampant in most major cities across America. A prime example of modern politics gone wild is a California Congresswomen calling for the harassment of Trump supporters, actually yelling it to a group of protesters. This type of behavior from a congresswomen is totally unacceptable, as well as dangerous and barbaric, and on national t.v. But she remains in office with absolutely no repercussions. How is this possible, if it was me or you, we would be in jail.

Selfishness and greed go hand in hand with addiction. Look around, it's everywhere these days. Just throw in a little dysfunction, hate and unrest and you have an addict, or just about any major city in America. As shocking as it is, this list was born out of the seven deadly sins! Some may say, "well that's religious and I don't believe in that.", but you don't have to believe in religion to feel that lust and greed are bad. You only have to be morally civilized. As addicts, we have no morals, only selfish desires, and we don't care if we have to break the law to get what we want. As long as we get it. Nothing, I repeat nothing else matters, only us and our feelings. This is the typical mindset of an addict, and a lot of politicians these days.

So, it's working its way, or has been working its way through our government at an alarming rate. Famous pedophiles and rapists as well as con artists rubbed elbows with at least two of the last three administrations we've been through here in America. Call me crazy, but I don't think this will sit well with most people. These people have gotten away with murder, rape, money laundering and embezzlement, just to name a few. I can't remember a time when D.C. wasn't corrupt. Except maybe during Reagan's tenure. It's sad to say that there are still politicians actively working against the American people who have been there that long. Most dogs don't even live that long! It wasn't until a political outsider was elected to the white house, that we could really see what's going on. Our great President cannot be bought! Oh, what a joy to the American people. Now can these career politicians finally pay for what they did in their insatiable thirst for power and money? But no one can ever pay back for a life that was taken. All too often people were found who "suicided" themselves all the while being whiteness to murder or other political wrongdoings by the rich and famous. Or our kids miss out on a college scholarship because some TV star bought her daughter's way into said college.

For literal generations, the American people have suffered under the increasingly crushing laws imposed only upon us. Not them or their famous friends. We are the ones who go to jails and prisons. They send our children to go fight their wars, not their children, they get million-dollar jobs? Now that we have an A.G who isn't afraid of his own shadow, maybe something will get done. But that remains to be seen, after a lifetime of being taken advantage of, not only by bosses, but by my own government as well, many people are skeptical anything will happen.

The United States of America was founded, and born out of Christian faith. No matter what anyone else told you. These are the facts. This is actually the reason our monetary system says in God we trust. And for good reason, this whole country, how we do things, and the reason behind it, is based on Christian faith. Being kind to our neighbors, helping each other out. Kindness and generosity are rooted in Christian faith. The true fact of the matter is, we advanced to where we are now only by our belief and faith in God. Christianity has taught that all men are created equal. This has obviously spurred growth in this country over the years and helped us develop into the nation that we are today. The underlying factor here is, God stands for all things good, love, hope and faith. While evil stands for all things bad, murder, rape and lawlessness. It doesn't take a rocket scientist to figure out which is best for us as a country.

Suffice it is to know how all of Hollywood is against our first ever un-selfish President, who has done tremendous things for America, unlike that of any other President in history as far back as when Ronald Reagan was in office, and still refuses to accept any salary. This is pretty big considering someone has already spent 2 million dollars of his own money just to get said job. It's easy to see their anger is purely ego driven, as these people are all about power and prestige. The ego is a tricky thing, I've struggled with it for years. As addicts, we all feel like we are better than everyone else. Especially the functioning addict. We know when to do it, how to do it, as well as who to do it to. And we would probably do a better job than anyone else. This is where the ego becomes our enemy, we become brazen and bathe in feelings of superiority. This is an all too easy life trap to fall into, but one that's emotionally difficult to get out of. Once stricken with this " mind-ride", the inflated sense of self takes over and can actually change your character. This can be seen most by the

Robert Christopher Padmore

people close to you, but can also be appreciated for what it is in sobriety, once self-honesty is present.

For anyone who has ever been a child (pretty much everyone), we all know how children act when they get caught doing something they're not supposed to be doing. First, they deny that they did it at all, then as time goes on, they go on to blame any and everything as a reason for this happening because it wasn't me. Or any one of a string of events leading up to this happening. This behavior needs to be analyzed when it comes to our representatives in congress, because these people are supposed to be of a nobler spirit than the common man. These people are acting like children in a playground. This is dysfunction at its finest. A symptom of the seven deadly sins. The proof is in the pudding, this is the swamp of D.C. This illogical and irrational behavior has become the norm after the last couple of administrations, and for sure has a lot of people ensnared, this is the real reason behind this resistance we're experiencing. These people have focused all of their attention for the last four years on hate. The average American worker doesn't agree with spending four years of their hard-earned tax dollars on a hate campaign.

But the average American worker shows up for work late three times, and are let go. They want us to shut up and go to work so we can collectively earn them their paychecks, while they talk down to us and steal from us. Let's be honest, if I went to work and stood around doing nothing, or even work on a project of my own, I would be accused of stealing time from my company, or riding the clock, as it used to be called. Now, let's put this into perspective and look at how these "representatives" of ours live and act. Personally, I feel a country as great as ours is should have representatives more "in touch" with the people, instead of being in touch with dysfunction, as this is a child's game

Addiction is the perversion of our needs and hurts everyone involved, even on a global scale. I think America being the leader of the free world should take some time and investigate addiction and corruption within it's own governing body. But, of course, that would be akin to bloodletting in their eyes. For if they have done nothing wrong, they should have nothing to worry about. Just like how they investigated President Trump for three years. Let's look at who called for these investigations in the first place, Representatives whose own districts have fell into disrepair and homelessness runs rampant as well as drug use and disease. All the while, the average American worker, who pays their paycheck, and is just looking for a better life for them and their children, gets to wallow in governmental regulations from a lost era, and has to deal with governmental obstruction from the same group of lost people.

CHAPTER FOUR

RECOVERY

Though the road to get here is rough indeed, vigilance must be exercised, as recovery has to be wanted, worked for and learned on a daily basis. As addicts, we are vulnerable in many ways. There are physical triggers as well as mental and emotional. This is in the forefront of our mind after dragging ourselves through however many years of addiction. We have to learn to live with a different mindset, our very lives depend on it. Remember when I said you need to have an open mind? This is where that particular mindset is most helpful. An honest look at ourselves shows we have a problem that we can't seem to fix. It seems so strong, almost like it's embedded in our very soul. And it is. If you've been doing it long enough to get addicted, it's already inside of you, and will never get any better. Problems only get worse until they're solved. Addiction is a progressive disease and will prove that point, if it already hasn't! The only thing we can do about it is to work daily against it. Much like A.A's way of getting sober. The 12 steps of A.A outline a spiritual path to be followed that is meant to get you sober and fix your life all at the same time. Though I didn't finally get sober in A.A, I spent a couple of years in the rooms, and it is a very good place to build a sober foundation for yourself. So, we have to believe in God? Use your open mind here, you only have to believe in a power greater than yourself! That's all, not someone walking on the clouds throwing lightning bolts at us! My opinion may be biased, however. I was raised as a Roman catholic, and identify as a born-again Christian. But I am a realist, I can see an engine as a power greater than myself, I can't run as fast as a car, or bust concrete as fast as a jackhammer. So, believing in a power greater than yourself is not a far leap of faith for anyone, to be honest. So, once we've identified the problem, and are past the God problem, (remember, we don't need to complicate things with beliefs) we are ready to work on ourselves, as this is where the problem really lies. First of all, the attitude and the emotions both fall under the realm of conscious awareness. That is, we're aware of a sudden attitude change, or that burst of emotion when it happens. We can no longer use our attitudes as defense mechanism or as a tool. In recovery, we are responsible for our own actions, it's fight or flight, no more co-dependency, as this will only keep us addicted longer. I believe most addicts have a 'who gives a shit' attitude. This is very problematic and this attitude must be harnessed tightly. Believe me, there will come a day when you will care, I can tell you that with as much certainty that the sun will probably rise sometime tomorrow morning. We are all human, no matter what skin color, nationality, creed or what have you. Addiction doesn't care and will accept the whole human race if we are willing to give it. And that goes for your frame of mind also, this too is personal experience. And as mentioned above, we are all human, it will be similar for you also. The change will start slowly, though sleeping is rough in the early stages of recovery, it does get better as time goes on. We will learn to take less risks, if any at all. We will actually feel ourselves slowing down, and be consciously aware of it (as addicts we have high blood pressure). Here we start to clear the stumbling blocks away as well as the mental smog we were in. A lot of emphasis is put on anger and self-righteousness. These feelings are mostly negative and have no place in recovery. Don't get me wrong, anger is a valid emotion and we will continue to feel it, however, it can't be used in a negative way, or in a way that will hurt other people. This is called mis-directed anger, and is a classic trait affecting addicts. You can see, the two only snowball off of each other and get worse. Another interesting point is H.A.L.T. This stands for, hungry, angry, lonely and tired. This, too, is a classic trait for us addicts, and when in the midst of any of these feelings\emotions, it will cause us to make bad decisions, and effect our ability to rationalize things.

After having to confront our ego for carrying on in such a dysfunctional and self-serving way, we must now harness it's power and use it to work for the new sober us. Since it obviously wasn't working the way we were using it (addiction is a disease of the mind), common sense will tell us that it should work just fine if we use it in the total opposite way! Exactly backwards! This is totally foreign to us and may require a leap of faith. Those involved in church activities or any type of A.A or N.A meetings will find this easier, as these places recognize the value of service. Yes, getting our ego under control involves work, not only mental work but physical work as well. Donating your time to help someone else, especially the elderly or disabled will be very rewarding to us. Instead of using all of our time and energy to make sure we feel good, in recovery we learn the value of helping others. It usually won't be long before we begin to like it, if worked diligently upon, and we wish to be normal again, we must learn to be selfless in our actions as well as our behaviors. This is the total opposite of selfishness and the only way to truly get away from it.

We must stay vigilant here. In extreme cases, the ego has grown and festered out of control for so long that vanity has actually become part of their soul. If you observe people, it's more than obvious, given the way that they carry themselves and speak to people. If you wish to recover from any addiction this mental habit must be broken, as it is self-serving and in direct opposition to recovery. For the common man\woman, the ego can become poison if left unchecked. Moderation is the key principal here. It's totally natural to love and care for yourself, most people do, but the ego can be very tricky, bringing some to the threshold of megalomania. You only have to be human to see this, point being; we are all human, and therefore all the same. People from different parts of the world have their own characteristics, skin color and hair, but these are minor physical differences. Underneath of our skin, we are all the same. People are fooled into thinking they are better than others, usually because they have more money than you, or a better job than you, or live in a better neighborhood than you, or practice better personal hygiene than you. Let us not forget the college educated liberal who still lives with mommy and daddy. The fact is, America has been slowly sinking into megalomania for years, this has been brought on mostly by the entertainment industry, Hollywood itself and how we interpret and internalize there behavior. However, this tragic case of monkey-see-monkey-do will only be passed on to the next generation for them to deal with. This is all the more reason for us to do something about this now, so our kids and grandkids don't have to live in a society divided by race, hatred and greed.

In recovery, we learn to slow down, no more running around all night trying to satisfy our selfish desires. We learn to be civil and have meaningful relationships, instead of our party buddies, who were always there when we were partying, but not for anything else. Slowing down and learning to live without active addiction is a process. I highly recommended meditation. Enough can never be said about this classic mind\ body exercise. Our brains are working all the time, every minute of every day, only downshifting to delta state as we sleep. Meditation and deep relaxation will help us to decrease stress lower blood pressure and bring a calming sensation deep inside of us. Something as simple as our breath can help us. Many people aren't aware of this, most people tend to be shallow breathers, what I mean by that is, a small inhale followed by a small exhale. This type of breathing is sufficient enough to keep us alive, but not sharp and on the ball. Deep breathing is associated with meditation and actually oxygenates your blood. This can be very helpful, especially in times of coronavirus, as your oxygen levels go up in your blood, this boosts your immune system, it also improves your digestion and reduces overall stress.

The truth is, we are all human and when dealing with addiction, we must realize how it bends our thoughts and twists our desires. In the midst of our addiction we cannot see this, as we only live for our addiction and nothing else matters. But in hindsight, it becomes quite obvious. As I've said, there will be many triggers along our path to sobriety. What it all boils down to is, how bad do you want to be sober\drug free? We are actually doing battle with ourselves, or that part of our mind that wants to keep us addicted. It's that part of our mind that we need to harness and use in, you guessed it, the total opposite way. There will be people indirect contrast as to how you feel about drinking\drug use, seemingly flaunting their dysfunction right in your face. These are the still sick and suffering addicts. As it's been said, misery loves company. All they really want is for you to indulge with them, so that they don't feel so bad about themselves. You probably have friends or relatives that at least drink. The most socially accepted drug in history. It can prove very hard for the addict to recover under these circumstances. This will of course make us want to drink, which for many leads to other things. If you're like me, one is too many and ten isn't enough.

We may have to distance ourselves from friends, co-workers and people perceived as friends. Let's be honest; a true friend wouldn't want you to be in danger of any kind. Friends look out for one another and only want what's best for each other. Getting into the behavioral aspects of the addicted mind, our brains work off of a reward system. That is, as we ingest alcohol, or our drug of choice, the chemical dopamine is released into our bloodstream, thereby bringing feelings of pleasure. Being creatures of habit, we like this feeling and want to feel it all the time. This is the part when the alcoholic or addict has the feeling of being unable to control themselves, and the urge is created mentally. Sometimes it's created sub consciously, that is, beyond our scope of perception, so we don't even know it. It's like our brain is a double agent and working for somebody else, and it is! It's doing what it has to do to keep feeling good. Here the addict is merely a pawn, caught between the almighty human brain and the painful, emotional, physical body.

Even if we wanted to stop, we can't. We tried detox, rehab, meetings, Church. We moved, changed jobs and girlfriends, even going to county jail and state prison over and over again, but we still used. This is the true malady of addiction. Even when faced with death itself, the addict seems to disregard it. This is, of course, the final and very advanced stages of addiction. But still and all, the very direction we are headed if we choose to continue to live that way. An obvious choice for most, but the addict is a true chameleon, able to blend into any crowd or situation, even go as far as to take up any cause and throw themselves into it, wholeheartedly, until their own demise. Many of us have painful emotional scars from sometime in our lives, whether the loss of a loved one or parent, a terrible childhood, a failed marriage or what have you, indulging in addiction will only add to the problems you already have, and will in fact impair your ability to make rational decisions in your life, causing us to experience unneeded stress brought on by the bad decisions we've made. And this is exactly what we must keep in the forefront of our minds at all times in recovery. We will never forget where we came from. This will in turn help us to feel more empathy and be more understanding of our fellow man. Especially someone who is experiencing what we have. This is a special relationship we get the opportunity to have, as someone else's personal life struggles are shared as well as the way we got out of them. This is actually the way I personally got sober. I accepted God into my life and began to pray for nothing but his will for me. I changed my attitude, my way of thinking and how I treated others. The biggest problem that you will run into trying to get sober is yourself. Some things in life require a leap of faith, and once taken, it will change your life in ways you can't even imagine.

....Poetic Ambience

This is a collection of poems I wrote when getting sober in prison. The previous four chapters were recently written. These poems are as true to life today as when they were written 2010-2013. They are not hard to read. some are funny, some serious, but they all have the common thread that runs through all of us, life experiences.

HATE TO LOVE

What is this world coming to, and just why are we here?

Learn to let go and let God, you'll have nothing to fear

The almighty dollar we worship, slaves to work and lust

To fight each other, live in stress, till we're turned to dust

It's not too late to figure out

God's will is so much more

We need to turn from hate to love

In our lives, his will can pour

The attitude in life, in the world which it stands

Is so very toxic, put yourself in God's hands

In God we trust it's said, but is it how we feel

The way we carry on sometimes, things tend to get unreal

We should unify ourselves, learn to live as a whole

Pray for God's will every day, that's a worthy goal

THE GRIND

At this point in my life, I've done a lot of things

Met a lot of strife, to this, me it brings

Stop the bullshit, no more insanity

Why are you pitching a fit, that always ends in calamity

Learn from your mistakes, make peace with your past

Do whatever it takes, and let's do it fast

Life is only so long, could be your last chance

So stop doing wrong, for once make a stance

Be helpful and humble, everyday that you live

This ball you can't fumble, to God, your life give

Live at peace with yourself, and soon you will find

Good fortune and happiness, stop living the grind

SELFISHNESS AND HATE

The world's biggest blunder is me, me, me

It's no wonder why we can't see

The pure selfishness growing deep inside

And the relentlessness that we peruse with our pride

It all starts with us, in everyone's heart

Stop causing a fuss and do your part

Let's rid this land of selfishness and hate

Everyone please lend a hand, before it's too late

EGO CHAMBER

Locked away in the vault of mind, only for our eyes to see

All our secrets are outlined, to ourselves we're carefree

Doesn't matter what people say, the ego hides in obscurity

And much to our dismay, we battle it with maturity

The ego will fester, like that of a child

The twisted court jester, because it's never mild

The ego 's a monster, grown deep inside

Supremacy is conjured, life's little joy ride

Full of the self, we cannot see

You're not yourself, an I Whoopi?

The ego can kill, best to keep it in line

Or your feelings will distill, and house in your spine

Robert Christopher Padmore

THE FLAME OF ANGER

No one can deal with feelings

The emotional turmoil inside

Somehow the brain stops working

This is just how we replied

Our mind jumps to conclusions

We fabricate all too fast

Even though our minds are biased

It's a feeling we can't get past

Consumed by the flame of anger

Sometimes we rant and rave

It's like the road to insanity

That with our anger, we pave

I've had these feelings all my life

I've studied them inside and out

They truly are a waste of effort

Take it from me, without a doubt

Time is too precious to waste like this

And our feelings offer no compensation

Nowadays I experience bliss

through prayer and meditation

HINDSIGHT

To look at things after they happen

Is to learn and see and grow

Its almost like a slap in the face

What you reap is what you will sow

Typical people don't think of this

As they go about their way

Living by the will of their own

While karma builds everyday

They don't know it themselves

How it affects their being

About how they live their life

Until through hindsight, they're seeing

The wrongs of their past

Things they should have done

By then it's much too late

Because now karma has won

ITS ALL ACCORDING TO HOW YOU FEEL

Do as I say pheasants, for the land goes by my rule

Bow to the diminished icon, for 8 years you've been a fool

Robert Christopher Padmore

Though life for me, hasn't been that great

Engaged in self destruction, myself I began to hate

Just hear my thinking, listen to the sound

From deep within, the true self can be found

To all those people, who say keep it real

It's all according to how you feel

If you're feeling you've been treated unjust

Maybe it's your pride, greed or lust

Everyone has a bad day, this we see

Pray to the lord, get down on one knee

Live life humbly , and never shall you steal

And remember, it's all according to how you feel

PARADOXICAL PLUNDER

Though it doesn't make sense, yet it happens to be true

Sometimes we can't believe it, like we never had a clue

But there it was, in front of our eyes

Like it shouldn't have been, just a bunch of lies

How do we accept it, how do we learn

To go against common sense, yet for knowledge we yearn

The question of the paradox, shall always be seen

If we sharpen our wit, and our minds are keen

So never give up, fight the good fight

And deep within our hearts

We knew we were right

BALLAD OF ANGER

With hatred in my heart, a good insult in my brain

I'm so comfortable with anger, it's really hard to abstain

It gnaws at my spirit, controlling my very being

How it hurts me inside , is what I'm not seeing

A true waste of time, and energy at that

People's feelings are the ball, my vengeance the bat

What does this accomplish, at this time today

Because of all of these feelings, at some time I'll pay

With my peace of mind, and stillness of heart

Today I will concentrate, and vow to make a start

To treat people better, as I'd have done to me

And one day my spirit, from anger is free

THE FUEL OF RAGE

Anger effects us in many ways

In ways we can't even feel

Robert Christopher Padmore

Sometimes we get lost within it's grip

Consumed in it's passion, we reel

Like a moth to a flame we can't resist

The emotions are reacting inside

Most times we embrace it wholeheartedly

Along comes dysfunction for the ride

In the grips of this, few can oppose

The true carnal feeling of hate

Almost euphoric we ride the wave

Rage is the fish, and we are the bait

Instead of all of this happening

And digging ourselves into a hole

We must first find the source

To do that, look in your soul

LOOSY

The changing of emotions, happens without a clue

Life's little explosions, the mind's fond adu'

For if it's loosely wrapped, and goes about unchained

In this world you're trapped, until you go insane

There can be no flaw, in the frame of mind

Or you will be in awe, with what you find

I am no dr.Seuss, believe me my friend.

If your mind is loose, it will spell your end

PEOPLE WHO ANNOY YOU

They are everywhere in life, there's no getting away

They always want to argue, no matter what you say

The people who annoy you, are every race and creed

Always having a bad day, to make you miserable, their need

They know nothing of karma, let alone how to live

They seem to get enjoyment, from the hard time they give

But as they do to you, they will get it all back

In one way shape or form, they will catch some flack

Like the universal truth, of sowing and reaping

As you do unto others, in that you'll be steeping

Until they figure it out, and take the subtle clue

They will always be that way, they're people who annoy you

THE CELL

These feelings forever burned into my soul

I struggle as I try to gain control

Pushed down and out, all of my life

Robert Christopher Padmore

Against my throat, I've felt a knife

Brought upon myself, all that I've done

Going to prison, boy this isn't fun

And now you shall receive, until you have learned

Now property of new York state, the title you've earned

Here's your cell, and something to eat

It's dark and gloomy, and smells of feet

I only drank a beer, and got in a car

Now I live in fear, my record is scarred

A piece of humble pie, for you my friend

Always stay out of trouble, it's a dead end

SPIRITUAL SPONTANEITY

Things happen for a reason, the spiritual world is connected

To the world and of the season, though it seems unaffected

Seemingly chance happenings, occur instantaneously

God's little scatterings, applied spontaneously

See more of you believe, the soul is full of truth

Reach deep, you can retrieve, to yourself be a sleuth

As it's been said, the truth is inside

Just use your head, let your feelings subside

relax and look deep, inside of your mind

in consciousness you'll steep, see what you find

CHANGES

The changes in life, though subtle indeed

Happen without warning, these words you should heed

As life consumes you, you go on your way

Thinking not of trouble, or how life can decay

For many many years, this has come to pass

It happens to everyone, just watch your ass

For wherever you go, change is always near

There's no need to panic, or cause any fear

Trust in the lord, follow your heart

Let's all help each other, that would be really smart

UNIVERSAL LAWS

Compassion is the key, to love and understand

Always do for others, all that you can

Helping someone brings contentment, into each of our lives

With this small act of kindness, it's karma that it buys

You must believe in your heart, this very simple clause

Or your life will be crushed, by universal laws

Expand your thoughts on cause and effect

Don't let it be yours, whose life will be wrecked

Not made by man, but by the supreme

Just open your eyes, you'll see what I mean

Everything comes full circle, to each and his own

And it's all up to you, how to the world you'll be known

ATLAS, HERE IS THE PROBLEM

Everything starts in our head, the possibilities never end

But when thoughts mix with emotion, that's when they start to bend

Most times it starts out good, but ends in what we crave

Our thoughts spiral out of control, we're lucky we're not in the grave

This formula can be applied, to all levels of thought

That happen throughout life, when in our own trap we're caught

Though self serving, most of the time

Our imagination is the box, and we are the mime

Through self discovery, looking deep within

Atlas here's the problem, of course it's sin

A life of contrition has now come to you

The ball's in your court, choose well what you do

WHAT HAPPENED

Nothingness is a disease, in and of itself

It will consume your very soul, since it moves with stealth

To take away hopes and dreams, fill the void with despair

It's home is laziness, soon you won't even care

This epidemic is among us, it lurks in the mind

The trick is recognition, then keeping it confined

It will always bring trouble, boredom and discontent

For these are the attributes, to you it has lent

LITTLE MUSES

The Muses of poetry it's said, of art the grand personification

They speak to me in my head, and give me an inclination

To craft these words in a style, make you think, make you smile

Reflect a little, look inside, never belittle, you decide

Life is about love, no matter what they think

Ask the Lord above, his eye will wink

It's what's meant for man, in conjunction with joy

Your life will be grand, good feelings you'll employ

Learn to live harmoniously, the rest of your life

We can all live jovially, just loose the strife

Robert Christopher Padmore

PERPETUALLY PISSED OFF

Narrow minded is how they are, full of anger and hate

They always seem to be annoyed, maybe it's a personality trait

I'm speaking of one kind of person

The kind that's perpetually pissed off

Life is so hard and full of disappointment

They come across as anything but soft

What happens to us is our own fault

We're a creature of our own making

Take your time, think things through

Your future you won't be forsaking

These words are tried and true

Believe me, I've been there

Live your life honestly and faithful

There will come a day you care

WHAT I NEED

Though it seems to be one thing, turns out to be another

Of all the things I think I need, it really is my mother

Who was taken from me, by a dreaded disease

It lasted a lifetime, only her did it please

Things are different these days, with God on my side

I pray with earnestness, now he's my guide

But my faith in him, was instilled by mom

My mind is now peaceful, and the day's are calm

I've been given what I need, every single day

The lord is my creator, and I am his clay

Who could ask for more, than what I've been given

A lovely wife and kids for whom to earn a livin'

YOU CANNOT RESIST

Drunken with demonic ways, people sow seeds of hate

Bubbling over is their glaze, an unfortunate personality trait

Your deepest thoughts given a twist, succumb to them you must

These dark sensations you cannot resist, until life becomes a bust

I tried to live in evil ways, it was all just about me

I've learned this lesson for many days, I try to help others to see

The only true glory that you will find, is buried beneath the hate

To unlock it the key is your mind, and higher knowledge the bait

Robert Christopher Padmore

PO-PO

The men in blue have a hard job to do

With society and what they hold dear

But do their jobs they must, with only God to trust

Just imagine their level of fear

To deal with the worst, your bubble they'll burst

When the cuffs go on your hand

Your feelings mean nil, you've abused free will

Prison is the hourglass and you are the sand

But this you can skip, with a stiff upper lip

Just use common sense as your guide or

Turn to religion, you'll be forgiven

And on earth you'll have a smooth ride

KARMA

People are very different, look around and you'll see

How many shapes, colors and races people can actually be

Present yourself with dignity, though this should already be known

Pride and anger are worthless to us, let it be and to each his own

It's been said before, with the heart we give

Just a small kind gesture, that effects the way we live

Giving brings good feelings, in resentment and anger we take

It's this heat of the moment, in which our futures we make

So be kind and give to all, let karma have it's way

For it will be returned to you tenfold some other day

REFLECTIONS OF YOUR HEART

Your truest of true, that only you knows

Is held within your soul, but through your eyes it shows

How you think life should be, is a reflection of your heart

After all our pain and suffering, from these feelings you can't part

It is the essence of you, like a beacon in the rain

Weathering any storm, though sometimes we complain

Like the history of man, we're never really happy

We want everything now, and please make it snappy

Dysfunction crowds our life, turning it upside down

We never get what we want, it just makes us frown

Prioritize your feelings, what really matters to you

Count your blessings, let your true self shine through

Do yourself a favor, get it right from the start

Always be true to you, these are reflections of your heart

Robert Christopher Padmore

ADDICTION

How can I deceive you, my troubled and twisted mind

You were once without a clue, till on my destructive path you signed

Through hell and high water, I've dragged your very soul

And almost to your slaughter, you've paid a heavy toll

Until the light of recovery, entered into your being

With the rays of discovery that you are now seeing

Put faith in the lord, take nothing for granted

Use the past as your sword, your world will be enchanted

To know oneself is key, align yourself in that direction

With your minds eye you'll see, scrutinize with deep introspection

Once you uncover the truth, from deep within your mind

It doesn't take a sleuth, to see what's been confined

ME MYSELF AND I

Hello my friend and welcome, to the theatre of my mind

Where thoughts are in abundance, only peace and love you'll find

I learned through repetition, that good will always bring good

There's a part within our minds we can sharpen, when understood

It's been stated in the bible, and in many books of lore

Every thought starts with a seed, but it must be honorable for sure

If it's not you'll soon see, thoughts and deeds seek their own kind

But it's too late when you notice, and to the undesirable you'll bind

That's the wrong path to take, I'll tell you because you will find

A life of trouble and much unrest, has all started in your mind

IN GOD WE TRUST

Take his hand, and trust your heart

From his eternal love, we cannot part

Satan is our enemy, he hides within our fears

So let God drive your life, use your faith as the gears

If no one has tired it, it wouldn't be known

Give your will to him, a better life you'll be shown

Put an end to unfaithfulness, angry hearts and greed

Get on board with God and love, make it your trusty steed

The only other way to live, is by our own sheer will

Without a higher power to guide us, chances at survival are nil

This country was founded for God, not for greed and lust

That's why our monetary system, says in God we trust

THE LORD

The lord works through me, in mysterious ways

Pointing me in the right direction, after all these days

I thought there was no one, gave up didn't care

Till one day I turned to religion, but how could I dare

To leave the old me behind, and find myself anew

To pray for love and guidance, and all I can do

To help my family, and all of my peeps

Show love and admiration, in great big heaps

Help my fellow brother do all that I can

Have a good time, create my own brand

There's more to life, than drugs and booze

If I continue that way, I'll surely loose

The love of myself, the respect of my kids

Then I'll end up on another of these bids

Giving time and anguish to the state

It would only be myself, for sure I'd hate

So I'll give all that up, and turn to the lord

Or I'll end up in a cell and be real bored

NOURISHMENT

Why do some people hate, you see it in their eyes

The soul's literal gate, from inside it cries

Oh to express gratitude, when I'm feeling pain

I lack the solitude, I just want to complain

Our souls need nourishment, with prayer and meditation

To reach the embellishment, of human adaptation

It's not really hard, loose hate and envy

This we must discard, to be real friendly

Have a little compassion, for our fellow man

Love is now in fashion, at least that's my plan

SHOW ME THE WAY

The doors of perception, for those who ask why

Are forever changing, till the day that we die

In the days of our youth, searching for identity

Lost and misguided, not knowing serenity

Feelings are burning, we must communicate

No one cares, time to emancipate

Moving up in years, into the middle age

Many aches and pains, at this life stage

As life goes by, we struggle to be heard

Things begin to happen, our soul's become stirred

We fight for justice, for our fellow man

Calling out all criminals, in our life span

The search for truth, seems will never end

Robert Christopher Padmore

That's why I don't watch news on CNN

As we age, so we shall learn

Careful your ass don't get burned

Be true to your thoughts, and that of your being

And through new eyes you'll be seeing

Thank the Lord for another day

And ask him please, show me the way

THE HAMMER

Rhymes are spinning, inside of my mind

Mingling with others, what will we find

The hammer of justice, most people know

Goes by thou shall reap what thou shall sow

But this doesn't happen, to the famous criminal

We go to prison, their punishment is minimal

But will the hammer, ever get it's turn

For those burned, oh how we yearn

But truth and justice, never prevail

Celebrity criminals don't go to jail

They make the news, and spread the disease

And America eats it up, give us more please

Are you kidding me, you can't be serious

I don't care what they say, they're obviously delirious

This I will say, and I hope you all listen

Break the law in America, and you go to prison

For justice to prevail, the hammer must fall

And crush their life, whether big or small

WAYS TO SAY GOODBYE

A thought that lingers, a moment frozen in time

As I embrace the darkness, that feeling of sublime

Taken away forever, and I don't know why

As I search for ways to say goodbye

I've emptied my soul, unto others fears

With no one to help me wipe my tears

My feelings I've cast out, a delirious solution

Still I have feelings of retribution

Though I grew wise in many of God's ways

My faith in as much, has grown these days

When I think of you, I will always draw a sigh

Until then, these are ways to say goodbye

Robert Christopher Padmore

THE SCATTERBRAIN

Life in disarray, thoughts in a jumble

Always superior, never humble

The need for speed has got us all

Today the scatterbrain walks tall

Running the business, answering the phone

Immediate attitude, loves to moan

People like this, always chasing their tail

Creating the situation, then loves to bail

Instigators are some, most can't abstain

Ladies and gentlemen, the scatterbrain

It's never my fault, it wasn't my mistake

Their very own soul's, they forsake

Creating their world, inside of their head

Me, me, me, everyone else is dead

The house of deadly sins, is their lair

Selfishness and deceit, becomes their mare

A life of entitlement, things never change

Bending reality, until it's deranged

Their vanity unreal, they live to complain

Always out of touch the American scatterbrain

REFLECTIONS OF ADDICTION

The seeds of unhappiness, like any other fruit

Through sowing and reaping, life will follow suit

From within comes the fault, for which you must deal

Be careful the answer, your very soul it will steal

Caught in this trap, there is no escape

Your senses are unreal, your consciousness it will rape

The only way out, of this awful place

Never have doubt, look for God's grace

The answer is inside, the key is your mind

From the truth don't hide, and the answer you'll find

ANGER

Anger is an illness, that hurts us deep inside

When we try to justify it, to ourselves we have lied

It always fuels our wars, at the heart of bigotry

Whenever we use it, it ends in misery

But anger brings a twist, in many different ways

It masquerades as hatred, which we know, never pays

Anger is part of our culture, it's roots are deep within

There seems no way to break it, we're stuck with this deadly sin

Robert Christopher Padmore

How about make love not war, seems a thing of the past

We really need to love each other, and have peace on earth

At last

THAT OFFENDS ME

Why in the world, must everyone lie

The major religions, even government can't deny

The need for deception, is really that great

To hurt all the people, cause everyone to hate

The demise of the intellect, at the top of the list

Let's protest everything, to this we insist

But this will solve nothing, as you all shall learn

You'll end up with nil, your own asses you burn

Do yourself a favor, don't incite a mob

Take care of your children, and go get a job

THE MIND RIDE

Concentrate on your breath, empty your mind of thought

Do this everyday, if peace of mind is sought

Listen to your heartbeat, and everything inside

Never be distracted, while on the mind ride

This quietude of soul, is what we should all feel

If deep within our hearts, we wish to keep it real

We know the mind is a muscle, do this to work out

If you wish to build serenity, this will without a doubt

It's also called meditation, the new mind body craze

I really suggest you try it, cause in the end it pays

FAITH

Transcendence is possible, through the mind's eye

It takes patience and understanding to know why

The natural force in life, can be daunting

If out of tune, your life it's haunting

This is the spot, for years I've been stuck

It gave me an attitude, I was out of luck

The world was against me, this I know

With no one to help me, nothing to show

Fighting this beast, shall never end

Aloof in my stance, knocked around the bend

Shattered and broken, my life fell apart

I should have known it, right from the start

I picked up the pieces, got out the glue

Now, to put them together, if I only knew

Robert Christopher Padmore

I put faith in the lord, was him I did ask

Please show me the way, to complete this task

He will always come through, faith is the key

I hope it unlocks your word, as it has for me

THE LAW OF PAIN

The thing in life, we learn in our youth

We don't like pain, hey it's the truth

As we age and get bolder in action

What happens to us is just a fraction

Not looking for trouble, we try to abstain

Get ready to struggle with the law of pain

This we know we know for certain

We don't wish to be the one hurting

Do the right thing, stay out of trouble

Or you will find, that your pain will double

There's no getting out, once you've reached this place

Trapped in the system, a continual punch in the face

If this isn't for you, do the right thing

For the song of pain, your soul will sing

THE JEWEL IN THE CROWN

I really want to, but then I really don't

My mind says stop, but somehow it just won't

The battle rages on, inside my head each day

Most times I never know, what I'll do or say

And such is the life, of someone who's addicted

A life in disarray, thoughts always conflicted

But I'm in charge, this much I know is true

I'll trash all of my thoughts, put faith in what I knew

Before I morphed into, this demented state of mind

I used to love myself, and that true self I must find

It comes with introspection, into days gone by

To answer the burning question, why do I get high

Unable to deal with feelings, the ego gets in the way

Now a grown monster, it's this ego I must slay

If it happens to you, all the days you will frown

I hope this helps, it's the jewel in the crown

PERCEPTION

The way we see things, especially the way we feel

Has great effect on us, and in this we reel

We make mistakes in judgement, what we do and say

But on the same token, it's the price you will pay

For acting on a feeling, like no one really should

Just like the Hippocrates, that live in Hollywood

Bathing in their ego"s, the mind's emotional gate

Instead of entertaining, now they make us hate

But the stars of old, always had their pride

They used common sense, and faith as their guide

There's something to be said, about feeling as such

Without faith my friend, you've really nothing much

A lesson in life, is what you all need

We all know dysfunction, is in your creed

Hollywood is a blemish, on California so great

All those silly liberals, they just love to hate

GREED

The big problem today, that lies in the self

Is the compulsive need for more, even in bad health

It's become a characteristic, in everyone's soul

The chaotic search for more, seems everyone's goal

It drives our workforce, everyone's fingers to the bone

And all the while we're working, we carry on like a clone

People hate what they do, but don't really care

The way things are happening is becoming very unfair

To spell it out, the problem is greed

We ride this high horse, our faithful, trusty steed

And so we carry on, till the day that we die

We can't get away from this, it always makes me sigh

PLANTING THE SEED

Cut and dry is my style, your attention is stolen away

I'll be around for a while, in your ear these words I'll say

In a nutshell, are these seeds

Beware of personal hell, through actions and deeds

To learn a lesson is very wise,

Go to confession, in your own guise

To understand living, is to know true bliss

The key to you I'm giving, so be sharp don't miss

Be thankful everyday, treat others respectfully

Careful of what you say, live life objectively

Be happy and praise the Lord,

Learn to live in this fashion

No fighting, put down the sword

Robert Christopher Padmore

Make intelligence your passion

JUST ONE MORE

My mind aches with a dreaded disease

My soul yearns for one more please

Like a dog who can't stop scratching fleas

Or how a forest fire consumes the trees

I've been like this, from day one

One is too many, I should really have none

But just one more and I promise I'm done

Since I'm past the point of having fun

A mindset like this is really sad

Makes me think of dear old dad

All the beers and good times we've had

Ended with cirrhosis, and that was bad

But I went through it, came out the other side

I've ruined my life, to many people I've lied

To live this ain't easy, it's like fighting the tide

Until you give up, boy it whipped your hide

But you can change your life, with this very thought

And experience good times that can't be bought

Live your life truthfully, if happiness is sought

Honor the lord daily, and follow what he taught

THE DEPTH OF YOUR HEART

The power to change the world, lies in our very mind

Like the essence of an orange, is hidden in it's rind

Prayer is a powerful force, rooted in laws of nature

From God almighty comes the source, for his earthen creature

These words are full of jewels, for those of you who care

The rest are merely fools, to go against God they dare

Only you can believe, in the death of your heart

All the things you received, you've known from the start

By the world it's been known, by people who are smart

Let your talents be shown, and the depth of your heart

THE SHUNS

For your information, of this compilation

The way I see I write

Makes no complication of my representation

Of things I think are right

So it 's my proclamation, the world's emancipation

Upon hate the world seems bent

It's an indication of our inhalation

I'm sure glad Trump's president

To remedy this situation, for our stimulation

The common working man

it's a provocation across the nation

And United we shall stand

LET'S GET SOBER

As I come to terms with myself, through many years of pain

It really seemed like fun at the time, now it seems insane

Along with age comes wisdom, down to the very core

Though I never believed it, thought it all folklore

From the school of hard knocks, dad said I'd never learn

Life was one big party, the end was not my concern

But I proved him wrong, in all that he said

I've sorted through my problems, that are up in my head

And now clean and sober, my world no longer grey

I'm trying to help people, through the things that I say

So take this to heart, in a world that is yours

Use your mind in a way, that will open closed doors

BRAIN NUGGET

Enlightenment is achieved, in a spiritual way

It's in your thoughts conceived, reflected in what you say

I don't speak in riddle, only in simple rhyme

I'm just writing these poems, while I do my time

It's been such a vacation, I learned a lot of myself

And I'm slowly nursing, myself back to health

Soon there will be a book, full of delightful rhyme

Though I'm still writing it, just give me some time

It's full of peace and love, and God's own rule

But I'm really just writing words I think are cool

GOD'S WILL

I pray for God's will everyday and night

To give me the strength and give me the might

To change my life and accept my weakness

I ask this of my Lord with genuine meekness

Help me through life and in times of sorrow

It's not mine but yours who's will I must follow

But it's not complete until you submit to yourself

To God as you know him put your will on a shelf

Robert Christopher Padmore

Act with love and kindness to my fellow man

To follow Jesus's teachings anyway that I can

To keep myself in check for this I am liable

And if I ever need help I'll look in the bible

LIFE HAPPENS

As a child I was lucky

With how life began

As a teenager it got sucky

From myself I ran

I turned to booze to ease the pain

Drugs and good times the easy way out

Fueled my twenties, but still raising Cain

By now I forgot what life's all about

Caught in my thirties, I couldn't escape

Entwined in my soul, was a terrible fate

Standing in the courtroom, my mouth fell agape

Could I have become, an enemy of the state

Continued through forty, though no longer the way

Trying to get sober, if I only could

Now I praise the lord, every single day

For helping me change the way I should

It would never have happened, if it wasn't for him

I was tired of my life, my future was dim

Now that he's with me, I have nothing to fear

After all I've been through, this much is clear

RIGHTY TIGHTY, LEFTY LOOSIE

Can you see through our lies, look past the corruption

Though we might seem unwise, we're all about obstruction

The constitution is just a paper, we really need no rules

Until you piece together our caper, we make everyone into fools

We have no message, we just want power

We're completely vestige, and don't care if things get sour

We're America's nightmare, with our freshmen how could we loose

Our agenda goes nowhere, and the speakers breath smells of booze

WHAT IT IS

Tears fall to the depth of my soul, anguish tears at my being

Lord knows this wasn't the goal, until through his eyes I'm seeing

The error of my way, greed and unrest riddled it's way through my brain

It was myself I came to detest, from alcohol I couldn't abstain

I accepted God, and for what he stood, then my life began to change

I learned to do right for everyone's good, suddenly I didn't feel. so strange

Free of the chains and constant oppression, a new face washes over me

No more lies or constant depression, through the lord now I can see

Armed with experience that comes with age, I have but one thing left to do

The only way is to make God your sage, and to thine own self be true

.......B.O.

Where it the justice, where is the truth

These lying scoundrels, really have no couth

If it's good for me, it should be for you

You broke the law, all the while you knew

The biggest lying scum, in all of the land

Forget the American people, we live by your hand

You destroyed the constitution, and true justice has ceased

You even went as far, as to endorse the hildabeast

The historic presidency, of the first black man

Was to screw all Americans, anyway he can

Please just go away, you racist piece of shit

Because without true justice, Americans will throw a fit

PRIDE

With grandiose behavior is how people act

Just watching them behave will prove that fact

The sense of self inflated, like that of a balloon

They don't really see, that they're such a bafoon

One of the deadly sins that grips us is pride

They treat others as servants feeling their acts bonafide

But it all comes back to you as you do unto another

Why can't we just realize, everyone is our brother

We're all God's people, with one worthy goal

To care for our families, until the final bell toll

PEOPLE ARE TOO DAMN POLITE

In such an environment, it seems to me

To be a requirement, to be as polite as one could be

It can be annoying, since we're all hardened men

To hear please excuse me, may I borrow your pen?

If you're so delightful, and fancy in taste

If just like to ask you, how'd you get in this place?

People act like gangsters, and say keep it real

But watch them and their actions, they don't know how to feel

The truth of the matter, we're all stuck in this place

But please just remember, I can punch you in the face

Let me just stop, as I'm sliding towards hate

Now I can identify my feelings, before it's too late

ARE YOU KIDDING ME

Each day is no different, just like the one before

When they lock you in a cell, everyday becomes a bore

I go up in my head, into scattered thoughts I sink

We're all locked up in our heads, with the crazy thoughts we think

The brain is the strongest muscle, in the universe they say

If we act on stupid thoughts, it's a severe price to pay

This is a serious poem, you shouldn't be slappin' yer knee

The thought that comes to mind, is are you kidding me

I try to deal with feelings, without going insane

I can't resort to violence, from this I must abstain

I have to use my mind, channel my thoughts, persevere

Once my head and heart is connected, I have nothing to fear

IT CAN HAPPEN TO YOU

This one is for all the girls, who should be treated as such

Like how an oyster holds it's pearl, with respect they deserve much

The holder's of the flame, a torch passed in life

Things are never the same, till we make one our wife

With love and adoration, confessed to one another

Through blessed cuplation your girl becomes a mother

With peace and serenity, you gaze at your offspring

And very gratefully, you accept God's offering

Now you're on a mission, to find a better life

But when jockeying for position, your soul gets full of strife

And while we all complain, life is just so hard

We must learn to abstain, our own life we marred

LIBERALS

Hatefulness dwells deep inside, weaving around their brain

Feeling our acts justified, why should we abstain

Wronged in the past, upon their shoulder a chip

Their feelings are Their mast, and their bodies the ship

Thrown in turbulent waters, their rudder doesn't work

The captain is shouting orders, oh boy what a jerk

How am I trapped here, and how do I get out

I'm so full of fear, I just want want to shout

The rules of the fight, in which we are engaged

Don't test America's might, we are becoming enraged

BORN AGAIN

We choose our attitude, we choose our fate

When we think with our emotions

With Destiny we'll have our date

To have it's wicked way with us

It's ourselves we begin to hate

Sometimes we try to numb the pain

Anger becomes our main personality trait

Blinded by feelings, restricted by pride

We think everything is o.k.

Until we learn by living like this

It's our own personality we slay

Living in this empty soul

Disillusionment becoming despair

How do I get out of this place

There is a way, but do I dare

The old way of life must go

To the Christ your life you lend

Feelings of hope and faith are ingrained

Why not become born again

When you need a change, a different perspective

Live for the true son of man

Everyone's accepted, for he's not selective

Live or die by your own hand

THE PARADOX OF DUAL SOULS

Why do bad things always happen, when it's happiness I sought

The shine of a fancy lover got my attention, and I was caught

A battle rages on for years, all happening inside my brain

The almighty human power, capable of so much pain

To fool oneself !f is one thing, to believe it quite another

I'd drown my feelings in alcohol, intoxication became my lover

With this warped way of thinking, so it became my life

The only one who cared, was my kind, sweet wife

She stuck with me all the way, most bad times some good

I vowed to quit the drinking, she knew I never could

Then one day something happened, fell into place and clicked

I learned it was my own mind, that I myself had tricked

The paradox of dual souls, is what was wrong with me

Robert Christopher Padmore

At last I've found the chain's, once I break them I'll be free

THANK YOU LORD

I'm all the day's of my world, you've been right by my side

Your love of me is unfurled, once I got past my pride

Your love knows no bounds, for this I am sure

You come out in my sounds, oh Lord you're the cure

Though I didn't deserve, your love helped me see

Though I hadn't the nerve, the lord came to me

Walk with me in this land, put your faith in me

Together everyday, let's help everyone to see

How good life can be, with faith in the lord

Change your attitude and put down the sword

PSYCHOGENIC

Like ripples of water, so our thoughts emanate

Until they reach the edges, it's our world these thoughts create

Always be positive and true, know the depth of your soul

Treat others with kindness, this should be everyone's goal

Make peace within yourself, it will shine in your eyes

Live a life of humbleness, not deceit and lies

A lot can be said, for the art of meditation

The restful alertness, and quiet contemplation

I've spent many an hour, in the half lotus pose

Until a veil was lifted, and a new mind arose

YOUR AIR

What is it about you, that keeps my heart in a knot

You always smell so sweet, your face cannot be forgot

It is more than what is seen in your face, lips or hair

The most striking thing about you, is that of your air

Like the aura of a candle, God's love shines in you

It sparkled in your eyes, and in everything you do

You marked my soul forever with your kind, gentle way

I will never again be the same, there's nothing more to say

I WILL OVERCOME

The cry of the soul, I just want to survive

Though I'm not whole, and barely alive

You won't break my spirit, that's mine to keep

I can adhere it, the benefits I'll reap

Bashed all around, attacked from all sides

Robert Christopher Padmore

Feeling spellbound, my senses collide

The hardworking man, cannot be outdone

I'll spread my wingspan, soar over everyone

Art with my hands, and art of the mind

Living God's plans, my life is intwined

To bring you this message, keep you intrigued

It's a little expressive, don't get fatigued

For years I've sweated, always the apprentice

But never regretted, the reward monumenous

Master of masons, of mortar and stone

To victory I'm racing, let it be known

WHAT SHOULD BE

This terrible world, in which we live

Is all about take, and not enough give

Live is about opposites, but what we really need

Is to live without anger, unjust-fulness and greed

What will we leave for our kid's one day

If we're full of corruption, untrustfulness and dismay

We should unite together in this country so fine

Learn to love one another, your neighbor and mine

We'll learn from the bible, like God said we should

Then maybe we can live, in a world focused on good

BEST FRIENDS

Life is so hard dark and complex

Days run together, on to the next

Cant wait to get out, to reach the end

Go back to my house, and be with my friend

Through thick and through thin, we've come a long way

The love I have for her grows every single day

She gave birth to my kid's, she's the center of my family

We'll be together forever, through any calamity

Through annoyance and infidelity, our love only grows

Down to bitterness and grieving, we're shown new lows

Grown together over time, through thin and through thick

That's my baby's mama, she's one tough chick

New editions to the family, my heart longs to see

And teach my children, to be all they can be

Our roles are defined through the people we've became

To love and support one another, in that there is no shame

We belong to one another, two soul's lost in love

Our hearts fused together, by the lord above

Our spirits fly together, through the earth and to it's ends

The one God made for me, that's why we're best friends

BOULEVARD OF THE BROKEN SPIRIT

No one ever brought me down, like I did myself

Through broken relationships, lost jobs and the like

I had it out for me, my true feelings out on a shelf

Self destruction was buried deep within my psyche

Though I knew it all, to no one I would answer

I was killing myself, the world at my fingertip

My disease was eating me, much like cancer

It was just waiting for one more slip

I was on the boulevard of the broken spirit

Though I didn't know it at the time

My body was crying out, but I didn't hear it

I built my own box, and I was the mime

Living like this, is really a shame

Day's drag on, I was going insane

And there was no one else to blame

The only thing left was to abstain

From controlling my thoughts, actions and deeds

I put all my faith in God, as nothing worse could happen

Today I praise the lord, and happily plant his seeds

I love riding in his boat, and grateful he's the captain

THE GIST OF IT

The tragedy's that befall us, are brought by the human hand

They say ignorance is bliss, and for that this seems the land

All this can be reversed, given the right state of mind

Happiness does come from within, try it and you will find

It's us who controls our behavior, not shame, pride or guilt

We all live within the walls, that in our heads we built

It's intellect over emotion, to thine own self be true

A lot of people don't get it, they haven't got a clue

This poem is to bring awareness, for those who do not know

If you seek it let me help you, a sacred path I will show

First, die unto yourself, be born again in the lord

Follow the teachings of the bible, in this your heart is poured

Never wander from the path, follow it day and night

To learn it use your mind, and your life will be outta sight

CULTIVATE YOUR MIND

I can see the world, inside of my eyes

All the people suffering, while we're told lies

Robert Christopher Padmore

Inside of my heart, I can feel the pain

Watch the distress, hear people complain

Living isn't easy, without a guide

We always cause problems, by misusing our pride

And of the grandeur, behind our eyes

Living with despair and lies

Trying to be more, than they really are

Truly missing the mark, by far

People don't care, look down their nose

Of personal vanity, they're in the throes

THE EVIL INSIDE

There is no rainbow, that spreads over you

If you fight the system, like women on the view

People love to cry, the perceived injustice

Protests they buy, please just bust us

The evil has bought out, your very soul

The devil has sought, you to be his troll

Giving in to desire, let it be known

Your soul is a liar, the door you'll be shown

To us you're no good, the American working man

You will get what you should, live or die by your hand,

THE ISMS

The life of an alcoholic

Through the guise of psychology

Can be quite symbolic

Like life's little Analogy

Or severely diabolic

Like liberal ideology

The disease of the Ism

Embedded in grief

Look into the prism

To catch the thief

It's really a mirror

Your looking in

It couldn't be clearer

Your full of sin

Stop being a slave

Wake up my friend

Or end up in the grave

Addiction spelled your end

Robert Christopher Padmore

ADDICTIVE BEHAVIOR

Addiction it seems

Lurks in the depth of mind

As we try to gain control

We leave ourselves behind

Then we turn to immortal beings

With the substance that we crave

Things are fine and dandy now

But to it, we become a slave

Engrossed in our own debauchery

Is how we learn to live

Uncaring and unfeeling

The substance drains us like a sieve

We go on for years and years

Living this dreadful fabrication

Getting high became a way of life

As well as my occupation

Until one day we stop to think

What happened to the old me

Seems I sold my soul to the devil

And he will forever collect his fee

We all must reach a point

When we're tired of all of this

Then we'll be reborn spiritually

And seek happiness and bliss

FUNNY AND IRONIC

The moments in life are amazing

Some worthy of trophy engraving

Are at times funny and ironic

Some might think totally moronic

Funny, but not how you think

Not ha-ha, but slightly out of sync

And ironic of that with a twist

Almost like God is in our midst

The fleeting thought that can't be conjured

Enveloped in this the mind will ponder

Life goes on, it stops for no one

Funny and ironic will soon owe you one

No introspective thoughts, deeds or actions

Negativity in life soon gains traction

Blinded with ourselves, feeling philosophical

The hammer then falls, how is this possible

The will of God is much more harmonic

Robert Christopher Padmore

The will of our own is funny and ironic

THE OLOGY'S

Through the guise of psychology

Comes this little anthology

Of how people love to hate

With a sincere apology

For the following analogy

Seems it is not too late

To offer congeniality

To America's ideology

In this land, oh so great

With proper theology

And guided sociology

May the Lord become your mate

ALIGN UNIVERSALLY

I am only human

I do make mistakes

But with all of my troubles

I do have what it takes

To overcome the obstacles

My mind puts in the way

Because it gets restless

And just wants to play

To see through this veil

You must train your mind

Have pure thoughts and concentrate

This good will seek its own kind

The awesome power of thought

 Born in the soul of man

Has the power to change our lives

Be responsible if you can

It must align universally

With nature and the Lord

Please think rationally

Or you'll appear

out of your gourd

Robert Christopher Padmore

CPSIA information can be obtained
at www.ICGtesting.com
Printed in the USA
LVHW040748081020
668176LV00004B/533